Warrior Artists

Published by the National Geographic Society
1145 17th Street, N.W.
Washington, D.C. 20036-4688

Library of Congress Cataloging-in-Publication Data

Viola, Herman.
    Warrior artists : authentic Cheyenne and Kiowa Indian ledger art
drawn by Mark Medicine and Zotum / by Herman Viola : with
commentary by George P. and Joseph D. Horse Capture.
       p.   cm.
    ISBN 0-7922-7370-2
    1. Making Medicine. 2. Zotum. 3. Cheyenne art. 4. Kiowa art.
5. Red River War. 1874-1875. I. Making Medicine. II. Zotum. III. Horse
Capture, George P. IV. Horse Capture, Joseph D. IV. National Geographic
Society (U.S.) VI. Title.
    E99.C53M348 1998
    741.9′089′97078—dc21   98-2800
                                       CIP

First printing, May 1998

Printed in the United States of America.

NATIONAL
GEOGRAPHIC
SOCIETY

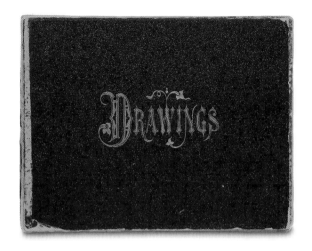

Warrior Artists

Historic Cheyenne and Kiowa Indian Ledger Art

DRAWN BY MAKING MEDICINE AND ZOTOM

BY HERMAN J. VIOLA

With Commentary by **JOSEPH D.** *and* **GEORGE P. HORSE CAPTURE**

Captive Artists, Compelling Art

BY HERMAN J. VIOLA

Hoping to quell Indian unrest on the southern plains, the United States federal government in the spring of 1875 imprisoned the leading warriors and chiefs of four tribes. The prison, Fort Marion, in St. Augustine, Florida, was half a continent away from their plains homeland. *Warrior Artists,* which reproduces drawings made by two of those prisoners, tells their story. One of the artists, Zotom (pronounced Zo-tamn), was a 24-year-old Kiowa. The other, Making Medicine, a 33-year-old Cheyenne. Between 1875 and 1878, these young warriors helped establish an extraordinary artistic community, and created a vibrant visual history of their life on the plains—a nomadic life based on the horse and the buffalo that was quickly vanishing.

The horse arrived in the Americas in 1493, as cargo on Christopher Columbus's second voyage of discovery, and by the early 18th century horses had reached the southern plains. Soon after obtaining horses, the Plains tribes also acquired firearms. This new and unprecedented combination of mobility and firepower fueled a startling social and technological revolution among the peoples of the plains, and predestined the violent encounters that would erupt as American settlers began to stream west after the Civil War to claim Indian lands.

The Arapaho, Cheyenne, Comanche, and Kiowa Indians were at the forefront of this conflict with settlers on the southern plains. The buffalo had nourished them physically and spiritually, and their young men gloried in combat. Life on the plains for these tribes was stable until American settlers arrived, bringing an end to their traditional raiding-and-hunting culture. By the Medicine Lodge Treaties of 1867, the horse tribes of the southern plains accepted reservations and agreed to stop their warrior ways. Nomads no longer, these once proud and fearless people had to submit to a new way of life they neither understood nor wanted.

Few had any realization what the change to reservation life really meant. The Plains Indians were suddenly dependent on others for food, shelter, and clothing, and were increasingly bored, depressed, and

Capt. Richard Henry Pratt and Cheyenne Indian prisoners pose for a photograph that would be sent back to their families as evidence of their safe arrival at Fort Marion in 1875.

Four of the 72 Plains Indians selected for imprisonment at Fort Marion would become ministerial students in New York State following their internment in St. Augustine. Posing for this 1878 photograph, they included Making Medicine, seated second from the left, and Zotom, standing next to him, third from the left.

COURTESY OKLAHOMA HISTORICAL SOCIETY

vulnerable to whiskey peddlers. As long as buffalo were available, the reservation Indians could hunt them, but it was clear to everyone, Indians and government officials alike, that the buffalo were doomed because of white hunters who slaughtered them by the thousands for their hides alone.

In the spring of 1874, pent-up frustrations exploded as Arapaho, Cheyenne, Comanche, and Kiowa young men retaliated. The Red River War marked a last desperate and hopeless resistance to the new order. From encampments deep in the country surrounding the headwaters of the Washita and the forks of the Red River in the Texas Panhandle, war parties went seeking revenge for real and imagined wrongs. The primary target was white buffalo hunters; some two dozen were surprised at their camp at Adobe Walls, a makeshift trading post in the Texas Panhandle, but the well-armed marksmen repelled the attack. Less fortunate were the unsuspecting and innocent farm families elsewhere that fell victim to the angry tribesmen.

The attacks provoked a prompt and aggressive response from exasperated government officials and embarrassed Army officers who thought Indian wars on the southern plains were a thing of the past.

Cavalry patrols aided by tribal members in the Army's employ scoured the plains in search of hostile Indians. With the buffalo all but gone, and soldiers at every turn, the war chiefs had no alternative but surrender. One by one the militants turned in their guns, and by the spring of 1875, most had returned to their reservations.

The Red River War was over. Determined to prevent future trouble, the government drafted a tough new policy designed to break the fighting spirit of these tribes once and for all. Those responsible for crimes committed during the outbreak were to be arrested and imprisoned in Fort Marion. Chiefs were given immunity for identifying fellow tribesmen guilty of crimes such as horse stealing, arson, rape, and murder, and assisted with the selection process.

In many cases the selections were arbitrary and capricious. On the Cheyenne Reservation, for example, a drunken Army officer lined up recently surrendered Indians, and to expedite matters "cut off eighteen from the right of the line," promising to review his selections at a later time. All 18 went to Florida.

One of the alleged Cheyenne ringleaders was Making Medicine. Zotom, the Kiowa, had specific charges against him: "Ze-tom (Biter) Was in party headed by Mah-mante, killing two men on Salt Creek Prairie between Jacksboro and Belknap, Texas, 1870 or 1871. Participated in the attack on buffalo hunters at Adobe Walls early in the spring of 1874."

Seventy-two Indians were selected for deportation—33 Cheyenne (including 1 woman who had killed a white farmer), 27 Kiowa, 9 Comanche, 2 Arapaho, and 1 Caddo. It was later discovered that of the Kiowa and Comanche prisoners, 11 were actually Mexicans captured as children and raised as Indians. In addition, there was Maltur, a Comanche mother, and her eight-year-old daughter, the family of Chief Black Horse. Maltur clung to her husband so tightly that the officer in charge let her join the group. Of these prisoners, ten died enroute to Florida or during the imprisonment. According to a report made to the Smithsonian Institution in February 1878, shortly before the 62 surviving prisoners were to be released, their median age at the time of incarceration was approximately 26. The oldest was 59, the youngest 16, and 11 were teenagers.

Among the prisoners were a few noted Indian leaders—Black Horse of the Comanche; Gray Beard, Minimic, Heap of Birds, and Medicine Water of the Cheyenne; Lone Wolf, Woman's Heart, and White Horse of the Kiowa. Several were guilty of heinous crimes, but most were ordinary young men guilty of nothing more than leading the traditional life of a Plains Indian.

The Army officer charged with delivering the prisoners to Fort Marion from Fort Sill, Indian Territory, was Capt. Richard Henry Pratt. Pratt had reentered military service after the Civil War as a second lieutenant in the Tenth Cavalry, a black regiment assigned to the southern plains, where he then spent the better part of a decade fighting the Comanche, Kiowa, Cheyenne, and Arapaho. He also worked with members of those same tribes as commander of a corps of Indian scouts. The Army ordered Pratt to escort the Indians as far as Fort Leavenworth, Kansas. Pratt, in turn, offered to take the Indians all the way to Fort Marion if he and his family could remain in the East for an extended period of time. In accepting his offer, the Army enabled Pratt to initiate

a remarkable and unique approach to Indian education that culminated in the formation of Carlisle Indian Industrial School, once considered by well-intentioned reformers as the ideal model for transforming reservation Indians into assimilated Americans.

The journey to Fort Marion took 24 days—by wagon, train, steamboat, and finally horse-drawn cart. Pratt reported the trip as uneventful, but he had his share of difficult moments. At first Pratt feared a rescue attempt because masses of angry men and anguished women and children, whose shrill wails wrenched the hearts of even hardened soldiers, surrounded the little caravan as it set out from Fort Sill.

After eight days of wagon travel, the Indians boarded a train at Caddo Station, Indian Territory. Upon arriving at Fort Leavenworth, the prisoners waited in the guardhouse for several days until word arrived that Fort Marion was ready to receive them.

Refusing to leave her husband, the Comanche chief Black Horse, Maltur and her eight-year-old daughter accompanied the warrior prisoners on the arduous 24-day journey to Fort Marion. The prisoners here include Black Horse, seated center right; his wife, Maltur, and their daughter, seated to his right; and the Cheyenne chief, Minimic, standing behind them with a bow and arrows.

COURTESY CASTILLO DE SAN MARCOS HISTORICAL MONUMENT

During this delay, Gray Beard, the leading Cheyenne chief among the prisoners, attempted suicide by cutting a strip from his blanket and hanging himself from an iron bar. Saved by his cell mates, Gray Beard, who had not been charged with any specific crimes, remained despondent. Later in the trip, when he saw Pratt with his six-year-old daughter, Gray Beard told him, "I have only one child, a daughter like yours. How would you like to have chains on your legs and be taken far from your home, your wife, and your child?"

Several days later, as the train slowed near the Florida state line, Gray Beard jumped from his train window. Although still in leg irons, the chief ignored an order to stop and was shot through the chest. He died two hours later.

Another casualty of the trip was Lean Bear, a Cheyenne chief accused of being a ringleader. As the train approached Nashville, he cut his throat with a penknife and stabbed two guards who tried to help him. Left for dead at Nashville, Lean Bear surprised everyone by surviving. When he rejoined the group at Fort Marion, however, he refused to talk or to eat, and soon died of starvation.

Adding to the trip's drama were the hordes of spectators who crowded the train stations in Fort Leavenworth, Atlanta, Nashville, Indianapolis, Jacksonville, and elsewhere, who were anxious to see and often—thanks to lurid newspaper stories painting the prisoners as savage beasts—to taunt the Indians. Near riot conditions prevailed at some stops along the route.

Little wonder then, as Pratt later remarked, that several of the prisoners drew pictures of the memorable journey.

Not everyone regarded the Indians as beasts. The writer Sidney Lanier, who witnessed their arrival in St. Augustine, observed only "proper men…weary and greatly worn [with] a large dignity and majestic sweep about their movements that made me desire to salute their grave excellencies. …[Yet] they are confined—by some ass in authority—in the lovely old fort, as unfit for them as they are for it."

The "lovely old fort" was the 17th-century Castillo de San Marcos, renamed Fort Marion. Today a national monument, the forbidding stone fortress, once the glory of New Spain on the Atlantic seacoast, was the government's prison of choice for particularly troublesome Indians. Among its celebrated occupants were Osceola and Geronimo.

Fort Marion may have been historic, but it was hardly an appropriate place to house 74 Indians for 3 years. No one was more surprised at its selection than the post commandant, Major John Hamilton. Three days after Pratt arrived, Hamilton sent a candid assessment of the situation to his superior officer in Louisville, Kentucky. The fort could provide only security, not comfort, he declared. He had originally been told just 5 Indians were coming, then it was 25, finally it was 63, but Pratt in fact showed up with 74 including 2 women and a little girl. "All this made great changes in the matter of preparation of cells, or casements as they may be called by courtesy." For three days following their arrival, it rained incessantly. Wood had been laid down in a couple of the casements, but the others had only "very dirty sand floors" made worse by the water leaking from the ceilings. "After such

weather as we have had, I believe all the cells leak at least a little, seeping through from the terreplein above." Another problem was heat. "It will be absolutely impossible [for the Indians] to live huddled in these cells during summer, without a possibility of a change of air." Hamilton had urged the construction of tent-covered platforms in the courtyard, but the Army would not bear the expense. Perhaps Pratt would have more influence, but for the meantime, "the Indians will continue to wallow in the filth of their cells."

Hamilton also complained about Pratt, who seemed to think he had an independent command. "He has been so long in charge of these men, that he considers it his profession, and them as his." The day after they arrived, for example, Pratt had taken the irons off six of the prisoners and escorted them all onto the parapet "to give them a view of the sea. Had I known," Hamilton declared, "I would have prevented it."

Although the Indians were prisoners of the Army, the Bureau of Indian Affairs was responsible for the expense of their imprisonment. Neither department was willing to allocate resources to make the prisoners more comfortable. In sending potentially disruptive war leaders to Fort Marion, the government had intended to encourage the tribesmen at home to adjust to reservation life; the prisoners were hostages to ensure the continued good behavior of those left behind. Beyond that the government had no interest in the welfare of these they had deported.

Pratt, however, was determined to rehabilitate these young men. In his letter accepting the assignment, he noted that few of the men selected for deportation were hardened criminals: "Most…[were] simply… following their leaders, much as a soldier obeys his officers, and not really so culpable."

Under Pratt, Fort Marion was not a prison but an army camp providing basic training to recruits. Within a short time Pratt had struck the chains from all of his Indian convicts, cut their hair, and issued them military uniforms. "It seemed best," he later explained, "to get them out of the curio class. There was some objection by them to these changes, but by kindly persuasion it was gradually accomplished." Wearing their uniforms with soldierly pride, the prisoners formed their own military company and became their own guards. They held their own military court and issued the punishments for infractions which violators readily accepted.

Indifferent government bureaucrats, cynical superiors, and insensitive townspeople (who welcomed the increased tourism the Indians generated but not their wandering the streets without an armed guard) could not deter Pratt from his efforts on behalf of his prisoners. Throughout his stay in Florida, Pratt peppered his military superiors with letters, memos, and reports keeping them abreast of the wonderful progress his prisoners were making while urging improvements in their care and their status. Pratt removed them from their damp casement cells into a large wooden barracks they helped build. The structure occupied the entire esplanade atop one of the prison's massive walls, giving the prisoners fresh air and splendid views of the ocean and countryside.

Discipline was but one facet of Pratt's program. He welcomed women from St. Augustine who taught the Indians how to read and write. Clergymen conducted weekly religious services, and on Sundays those prisoners so inclined could attend church in St. Augustine. Two years later, Pratt proudly reported that 47 of the younger men were receiving "good instruction" 2 hours a day, 5 days a week, and that upwards of 30 could use the first reader. "They are just in that state of advancement," he boasted, "where they can understand and make themselves understood, and their progress increases every day. The teachers are so interested in their work that all begged me to try to get them held longer that they might have the more pleasure of seeing their efforts more fully consummated."

Firm in the belief that an idle mind was the devil's workshop, Pratt kept the Indians as busy as possible. He sought employment that enabled them to earn money while in confinement. Their first tasks were polishing "sea beans," or palm seeds, and alligator teeth which local dealers sold to tourists. For polishing the beans which washed up on the Florida coast, dealers paid the Indians ten cents each. Later, when the Indians were allowed to do their own beachcombing, they collected, polished, decorated, and sold the beans themselves, earning from 25 cents to a dollar per bean according to its size and quality.

Twenty-one of the 22 Indian prisoners who remained east to continue their education pose for a portrait during the last days of their internment. All but two of these young men were Fort Marion artists. Making Medicine and Zotom stand in the last row, second and third from the right. With the men is Capt. Richard Pratt, standing in the second row at the far left.

COURTESY NATIONAL ANTHROPOLOGICAL
ARCHIVES, SMITHSONIAN INSTITUTION

The Indians also performed tasks in and around St. Augustine. They cleared brush and chopped trees, they toted luggage at the train station, and they made handicrafts. Especially popular with the tourists were bows and arrows. Some of the Indians also gave archery lessons. Pratt welcomed any task that provided the Indians with money while also teaching them something useful, provided the work was not demeaning. At popular request, he even hosted two traditional Indian dances and a simulated "buffalo hunt" as fund-raisers. As Pratt explained to anyone who cared to listen, he considered it the government's duty "to be the teaching of them something that will be permanently useful to them."

Government officials were unmoved by such sentiments, and were unresponsive when the Indians made their own appeals like the one from Chief Mamanti, a Kiowa prisoner, whose request Pratt sent forward in June 1875. "Tell 'Washington' to give us our women and children and send us to a country where we can work and live like white men," Mamanti requested. "There are a great many Indians at Fort Sill and in that country who have done more bad work than we have, and why should they be allowed to go free, and be happy with their families and we are sent down here as prisoners to live in these dark cells. That is not right."

Gen. Philip Sheridan dismissed Mamanti's eloquent plea as "mere Indian twaddle." All the Indians at St. Augustine, Sheridan reminded Pratt, "are unmitigated murderers of men, women, and children without a single particle of provocation." Nonetheless, in order to keep from being pestered by such petitions, he approved the request but only for each man's "immediate family circle."

The request was rejected by the Commissioner of Indian Affairs. Dismissing Pratt as "inexperienced" and endorsing Sheridan's notion that Mamanti's speech was "twaddle," the commissioner refused to allow the families to be reunited in Florida.

Mamanti died a month after making his plea. Its rejection was a bitter disappointment to both the prisoners and Pratt. "I do not forget that they have been 'unmitigated murderers of men, women, and children,'" he retorted, but having been the worst of their people because they were the most active, he predicted they would become the best of their people for the same reason, "if permitted and aided to it. It is protection to ourselves to open wide the door of civilization, and even drive them to it while we can, if we find that necessary," he advised. "But we will not find it necessary—they will enter of themselves. They may flag, but under proper management, will recover and push ahead."

Despite such disappointments, the prisoners managed to keep up their spirits and their art, which was more than a fortunate by-product of the effort to keep them occupied. Drawing, in fact, was as natural to these men as hunting. Before paper became available, Plains Indian warriors expressed their art in carvings, and on smooth surfaces such as bone, bark, rock walls, and tanned animal hides such as deerskins and buffalo robes. But once introduced to paper in the early 19th century, Plains warriors eagerly adopted the new medium for their artistic expressions. Since the first paper products usually available to them were the large, lined accounting books kept by traders and military officers, their wonderful, expressive creations are known today as "ledger art" even though warrior artists used virtually any paper products that came their way, including diaries, notebooks, army rosters, and business flyers.

The ability of Plains warriors to draw was widely recognized by the whites with whom they came in contact. Indian fighter Col. Richard Dodge, for example, declared: "All [Indians] draw, and though entirely without knowledge of perspective, all draw quite well as well as the average whites. If one wants pictures, there is no need to hunt a special artist. All he has to do is give some paper and a few colored pencils to any middle-aged warrior."

Although he seems to have viewed the drawings more as curiosities than art, Pratt made them part of his public relations campaign on behalf of his prisoners after witnessing the excitement the works aroused in visitors. Pratt gave the Indians paper, pencils, and inks and told them to draw. They needed little encouragement. During their internment the prisoners rendered hundreds of drawings and filled dozens of sketchbooks which they sold to tourists, clergymen, and other visitors.

An avid purchaser was Henry Benjamin Whipple, Episcopal Bishop of Minnesota. While living one winter in St. Augustine, he became a frequent visitor to Fort Marion and a patron of its graphic arts program, buying numerous drawing books for presentation to influential individuals as proof of the warriors' progress toward assimilation. "I was never more touched than when I entered this school," Whipple informed President Ulysses S. Grant. "Here were men who had committed murder upon helpless women and children sitting like docile children at the feet of the women, learning to read." In March 1876, Whipple asked Pratt for "one more copybook of Indian drawings and some photos of the Indians." The artists gave him the drawings for free. Several months later, Pratt informed the bishop that the artists "seldom make a drawing book now without putting you in. The Bishop talking to them, the classes and teacher and their lives as soldiers are three staple pictures. Several good books are in progress. Will send one when done." That November Whipple ordered five more books, but this time Pratt charged him two dollars apiece.

Besides drawing pictures for sale to tourists, many of the prisoners drew pictographic letters to communicate with loved ones at home. Immediately after their arrival, Pratt arranged to have photographs taken of the prisoners which he sent with their pictographic letters to the Indian agents at their home reservations. The packages arrived in early July 1875. "It would be very difficult for me to convey to you and your charges an idea of the joyous excitement produced in camp over the information of the arrival of their 'remembrances,'" responded John D. Miles, the Cheyenne and Arapaho Indian agent. "My office was soon crowded to overflowing, [all] anxious to get a glimpse at the faces of their loved ones, and to receive each his or her distributive share of the 'tokens.' Minimic's folks, and Bear Shield's wife were of the first to reach my office. …[She] said she loved Bear Shield & must have his letter. …Next came White Bear's (Arapaho) father & mother. I thought they would eat me up for joy. Medicine Water's folks were in the throng, in fact all were here but Grey Beard's folks. I do pity his wife. She can scarcely realize her husband is dead. …I think our Indians fully realize now the benefits of mail communication and if there is any one thing that they would fight for & defend it is our old mail coach. It brings them such good news. …P.S. Our Indians will send more moccasins whenever you say they are needed—or other little trinkets."

For three years, Fort Marion was a hive of artistic creativity and the fact that so many examples of the prisoners's efforts are extant today indicates the value placed on the drawings by the owners. One was Commissioner of Indian Affairs John Quincy Smith, the original owner of the art book reproduced here. Smith received his appointment from President Grant, a fellow

13

Ohioan, and was in office during a turbulent period that witnessed the Battle of Little Big Horn, the Ponca Removal, and the outbreak of the Chief Joseph War.

In February 1877, Pratt sent a lengthy letter to the War Department that included eloquent petitions by Making Medicine, speaking for the younger prisoners, and Minimic, a Cheyenne chief who represented the older men. The petitions were intended to remind government officials that the Indians now had been in prison for two years. They hoped to be set free or put to work at some occupation that would prepare them for life on the "white man's road." Pratt urged his superiors to heed their pleas. "All indications favor that the best results will follow clemency and practical assistance to these people," he wrote.

Commissioner Smith, perhaps moved by this letter, expressed interest in learning more about the status of the Indian prisoners. Pratt used the request as an opportunity to visit Washington and meet with him. It was most likely at this meeting, which occurred in April 1877, that Pratt presented Smith this set of drawings.

After three years' effort, Pratt finally prevailed on the government to free the prisoners. When time came to return them to Fort Sill, 22 of the young men chose to remain in the East. Five, including Zotom and Making Medicine remained for religious studies; the remainder, accompanied by Pratt, went to Hampton College, Virginia, a school for freedmen established after the Civil War. Pratt, however, feared the prejudice against blacks would extend to the Indians at Hampton, so he

Indian Sports and
War Dance.

Under the Auspices of the St Augustine Yacht Club.

Captain R. H. Pratt, U. S. A., has kindly consented to permit the Indians under his charge to give a war dance, in costume, and display their prowess with the bow and arrow.

AFTERNOON SPORTS.
(IN FRONT OF MARKET.)

Arrow Pitching and Archery. Over Thirty of the Braves will compete and pierce a target at the extraordinary distance of 200 Yards.

FORT SAN MARCO, 8 o'clock.
PROGRAMME OF DANCES.

INTRODUCTION   Cheyenne Walk Round.
Osage War Dance, (in which horses will be introduced.)
Kiowa Ring Dance.
The whole Troupe will be divided as follows :

Singers.

White Horse,	Aw-lik,	Buffalo Meat,	Little Chief,
	Tsah-dle-tah.		

Dancers.

1st Company.	2d Company.
Little Medicine, Capt.	Bear's Heart, Capt.
Tio-cea-kah-da	Nick,
Shave Head,	White Bear,
Wohaw,	White Man,
Wy-a-ko,	Ta-a-way-ite,
Cohoe,	Maw-ko-peh,
Toun-ke-uh,	E-tah-dle-uh,
Zone-ke-uh,	Packer,
Chit-taint,	Zotom,
Squint-Eyes,	Buzzard,
Chief Killer.	Rising Bull.

The Committee beg leave to announce that this will positively be the last public performance of the Indians.

ADMISSION.

Reserved Seats, (Red,)	50 Cents.
To the Ramparts, (Green,)	25 Cents.

The Fund raised by Admission to the Fort is to be devoted to the **EDUCATION OF ONE OF THE INDIANS.**

COMMITTEE.

Capt. R. H. Pratt,	Robt. D. Bronson, Esq
U. S. Army.	St. A. Yacht Club.

prevailed upon the Army to establish a separate school for Indians at Carlisle Barracks, Pennsylvania.

As for the other prisoners, however, Pratt's worst expectations were realized as they were simply turned loose with no direction or assistance. Left on their own, the former prisoners merged into the general Indian population on their reservations—Fort Marion and the white man's road a fading memory. When questioned about the Kiowa and Comanche prisoners after their return to Fort Sill—"whether these seem to have profited by the educational and civilizing opportunities their detention in St. Augustine has afforded them"— the commanding officer replied: "I do not think the extent [of their influence] amounts to much. Indeed, it is my impression these Indians have lost what influence they had. The St. Augustine Indians can write a few words, sing a hymn or two, but are wanting in a knowledge of the industrial pursuits of life. The consequence is they find the larger number of their tribal associates far better off than they are, and it would not be strange if they lapsed into their former savage ways of life."

Although few of the "Florida boys," as they became known, continued to draw after leaving Fort Marion, they created a rich artistic legacy while there. What makes this book particularly significant is Zotom's pictographic diary, which documents his transition from warrior to prisoner to soldier and to student.

"This man," Pratt later told Zotom's religious instructors, "for months after his capture was so perverse and insubordinate that it was almost determined to shoot him as an example to his companions of the necessity of submission to authority." Described as "headstrong and heartstrong," Zotom was blessed with multiple gifts. He was an artist, painting ladies fans and filling several sketchbooks with detailed drawings like the ones in the following pages. He was a musician and became one of the two Fort Marion buglers, later teaching the skill to students at Carlisle. And he was a dancer. He not only demonstrated his skills in the two traditional Indian dances held at Fort Marion, but he was also chosen by his associates to be one of two dancers to perform at a benefit held at a St. Augustine hotel.

Zotom had other attributes as well. According to sculptor Clark Mills, the young Kiowa was the finest specimen of a human he had ever seen. Mills was commissioned by the Smithsonian Institution to make plaster busts of each of the Fort Marion prisoners. Mills was so taken by Zotom he cast his entire body. According to the inventory Mills prepared for the Smithsonian, Zotom was 5' 7" tall and weighed 175 pounds.

The other artist represented in this book is Making Medicine. His Cheyenne name, *Okuhhatuh,* more accurately translates as "Sundancer," indicating that he was a person of great spiritual power. Making Medicine became one of Pratt's favorite and most trusted prisoners. He was first sergeant of the company of guards Pratt formed at Fort Marion. He was also one of the finest and most prolific of the warrior artists.

15

Zotom, the Kiowa artist, paints a tepee cover in Anadarko, Oklahoma, in 1897, for display at the Trans-Mississippi and International Exhibition. The tepees he painted remain part of the permanent collection of American Indian ethnography at the Smithsonian Institution.

The earliest known drawing book from Fort Marion is by Making Medicine, and an exceptionally large number of his drawings have survived including several books preserved in the Smithsonian Institution's National Anthropological Archives.

Instead of returning home when the government finally released the prisoners in the spring of 1878, Making Medicine chose to remain in the East. While a prisoner, Making Medicine had befriended the family of George Pendleton, a U.S. senator from Ohio. It was Senator Pendleton who later introduced the legislation establishing Carlisle Indian Industrial School. Alice Kay Pendleton, the senator's wife, bought some of Making Medicine's drawings and he, in turn, taught archery to Pendleton's daughters. When Making Medicine had the opportunity to receive training in the Christian ministry along with three other prisoners—one of them Zotom—the Pendletons sponsored him. Making Medicine honored the family by taking as his English name, David Pendleton Oakerhater.

In this book, Making Medicine chose as his subjects happy scenes of his former way of life. He sketched buffalo hunts, dances, ceremonials, and games. The drawings are not those of a demoralized, brutalized prisoner, but of a person who has been given hope and prospects for a better life. Missing from these drawings by Making Medicine and Zotom are the scenes of warfare that were the traditional subjects of the warrior artists of the Plains.

Making Medicine and Zotom, along with two other prisoners considered "the brightest and most promising of the Indians," were selected "at their most earnest desire, to become Christian teachers and ministers to their people" and were sent to New York, according to the *Florida Churchman*. Three months later, Zotom, signing his letter Paul Caryl Zotom, wrote Pratt: "[I] do not forget you. I loves you. …School good I think. …I not sorry and happy every day I study hard any thing Books." In another letter, he wrote: "I learn a better way. I remember all my Indian friends."

An assessment of Zotom and Making Medicine made one year into their divinity studies is revealing: "Tribal characteristics appear in them, and sharp distinctions in personal character. The Cheyenne is most retiring, and evidences the greatest native refinement. The Kiowa, stronger in body, has a rugged force about him that the Cheyenne is a stranger to. … The Kiowa, after his own kind, [is] quick to see, apt to learn, sometimes headstrong and heartstrong, is growing in his own way. …he will be the voice which shall tell out with all the grace of Indian eloquence the good tidings that are now coming to him, and through him to his people."

David Pendleton Oakerhater and Paul Caryl Zotom were ordained Episcopal deacons in a joint ceremony on June 7, 1881. They then returned home to spread the faith among their people. Making Medicine remained true to his newfound faith until his death fifty years later. He is not known to have made another drawing after leaving Fort Marion. In 1986, he was included in the calendar of saints of the Episcopal Church.

Zotom found the return to reservation life more difficult. An Episcopalian bishop who visited Zotom in 1889, reported: "He has evidently left the 'white man's road,' and returned to the Indian path." His opinion was shared by Smithsonian ethnologist James Mooney who, writing ten years later, announced that Zotom had "sadly fallen from grace." Mooney employed Zotom, whose weight had ballooned to 350 pounds, to paint the covers of a series of model Kiowa tepees for display at the Trans-Mississippi and International Exhibition in Omaha in 1899. This commission appears to constitute Zotom's only known artistic effort since his Fort Marion days.

Scholars have remarked on the fact that the Indian artists are not known to have drawn much once they returned home from St. Augustine. A logical explanation is lack of market. At Fort Marion there was a steady stream of eager purchasers for whom Indians were a novelty and whose artistic expressions made delightful and attractive souvenirs. At home most whites they met regarded Indians with disdain, if not contempt, and were unlikely purchasers of drawings. Without a market and perhaps without the funds to buy art books and drawing materials, it is not surprising that the Fort Marion artists stopped drawing.

Another question that has interested scholars for sometime concerns the importance of these drawings beyond their intrinsic value as examples of Native American art. "More than evidencing their skills at accommodation," writes scholar Jacki Thompson Rand, "the drawings of the Fort Marion prisoners speak of the artists' accountability to their respective communities, the resilience of Indian identity, and the subtle forms of resistance that carried Native America into the twentieth century." She sees the Fort Marion art as "nothing less than an incipient national literature." Others have seen it as a bridge between traditional art forms and the contemporary creations of 20th-century Indian artists.

The role of the Fort Marion artists is difficult to define. They did not form a school of artists. Only one is known to have done similar work after his release from prison. Their real impact is in the non-Indian world. Their work, which survives in hundreds of examples— in private collections, in museums, and as illustrations in books—demonstrates to the world that the Indian peoples of the Americas possess an inherent sense of beauty and harmony, and an artistic strength that transcended racism, adversity, and all the other efforts that conspired to eradicate their inner soul. Perhaps this is the legacy of Making Medicine, Zotom, and their fellow artists from Fort Marion. *Warrior Artists* celebrates the creative genius of this small group of men whose bodies may have been confined, but whose spirits remained forever free.

Drawings by "Making Medicine"
Cheyenne Prisoner.

Castle San Marco
St Augustine, Fla.
August 1876

Young Cheyennes.

YOUNG CHEYENNES

Making Medicine has drawn a group of young Cheyenne men, each wrapped in a different style of blanket. The multicolored blankets were usually Mexican in origin and were obtained through a complex trade network that originated in the south. The solid colored blankets with a strip of geometric patterns were characteristic of most Plains tribes. Beaded by the women, these "blanket strips" were made independent of the blanket and sewn into place. This allowed the strips to be removed and reused when a blanket became worn and tattered. A woman making a blanket strip worked within the artistic conventions of her tribe when she created the design.

Making Medicine demonstrated his considerable skills as an artist in creating this drawing. He has placed two horses opposite the group of men and added one lone warrior on the upper right, balancing the composition.

CAMP SCENE

The Cheyenne are camped at a fork in a river. Many trees line the river bank which Making Medicine indicates with the blue wavy lines moving across the page. It is summer. Each of the tepees has an arbor, a brush structure built near the tepee to provide shade from the sun; it also allows any breezes to pass through.

Tracks show that the hunters have been chasing buffalo on the far side of the upper river. Most of the buffalo have crossed the river; however, one has been killed. Blood flows from arrow wounds and from the animal's mouth. A wounded buffalo charges towards camp in angry pursuit of one of the hunters whose horse is trying to avoid being gored. Another hunter on foot runs for the safety of the trees.

The commotion has alerted the camp. Some people peer out of their tepees, others stop their activities to see what will happen. One man has grabbed a bow and points at the approaching danger, while another—indicated by the hoofprints coming from camp—has already jumped on his horse and rushed to the scene, hoping to kill or distract the angry buffalo before it harms the fleeing hunters or charges through the village.

Camp Scene.

AFTER THE ANTELOPE

The pronghorn antelope was an integral part of Cheyenne life, probably second in importance after the buffalo. The meat was tasty and sought after, and the animal's hide was used to make dresses and shirts. Hair was used as pillow stuffing, and horns were incorporated into warrior headdresses.

Catching pronghorns was difficult. The fastest animals on the plains, they were a challenging target for even the most accurate of archers. Before acquiring guns, the Plains Indians stampeded pronghorns into corrals and pits in their efforts to capture them.

The excitement, exhilaration, and frustration of hunting the pronghorn antelope from horseback is evident in this drawing. Making Medicine shows the horses stretched out in full gallop dashing after the pronghorns which jump and pivot like jackrabbits. The hunters use a variety of weapons: rifles, pistols, arrows, and even a lance. The arrows lying on the ground near the running animal on the upper left side of the drawing indicate how difficult it was to hit such a small target. Although one of the pursuing hunters uses a pistol, the animal has been hit twice with arrows, suggesting that Making Medicine believed that the bow was the more reliable weapon.

To the right, a wounded doe tumbles to the ground. The hunter on the opposite side of the pronghorn evidently speared it, and the tip of his spear protrudes from the animal's left side.

After the Antelope

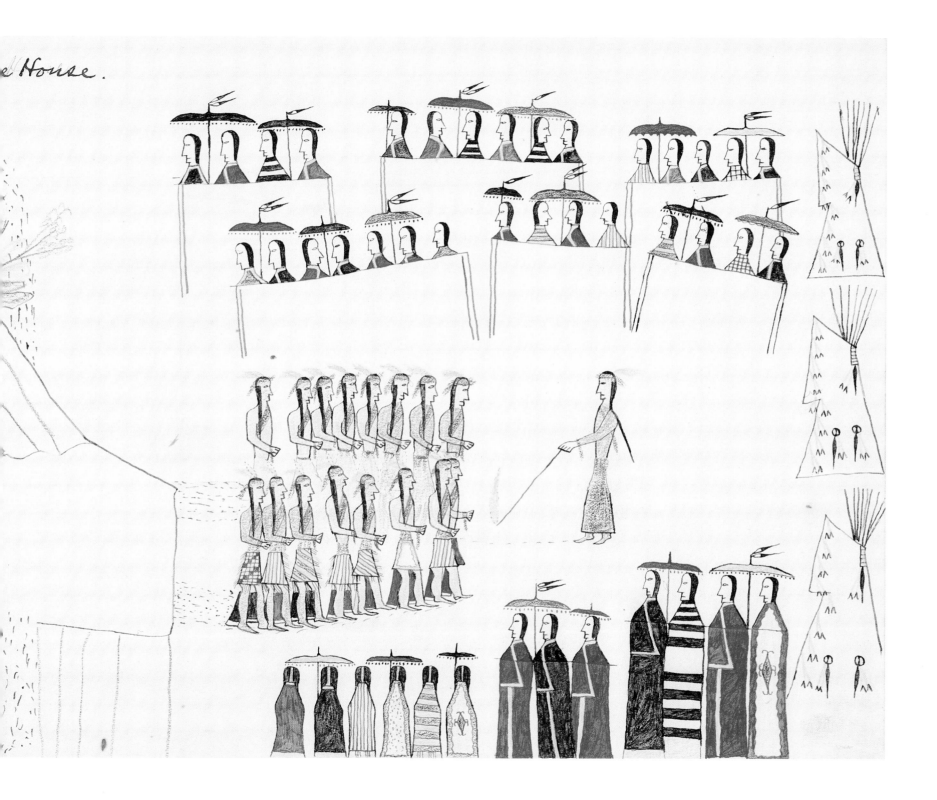

CHEYENNE MEDICINE HOUSE

Making Medicine acquired significant spiritual power or "medicine" during his experience in the Sun Dance lodge. This art provides a rare look at one of the most important ceremonial events of the Tsistsistas people, the Sun Dance. Roughly translated into English as "the real people," Tsistsistas is the traditional name of the Cheyenne.

Participants in the Sun Dance fast for several days and nights, offering themselves to the Creator. Sun Dancers paint their bodies and wear wreaths made of sage, continuing traditions that have lasted for generations.

In this drawing which spreads across two pages, Making Medicine illustrates the final moment of the ceremony. To the left of the lodge, members of various Cheyenne military societies such as the Crazy Dogs, Kit Foxes, Bow Strings, Dog Soldiers, and Elk Horn Scrappers watch the proceedings under awnings shielding them from the sun. To the right of the lodge, Cheyenne women and children look on.

The Sun Dance lodge or "Medicine House" serves as a temporary shelter for the Sun Dancers during the ceremony. In the middle of the structure a forked center pole holds the Sun Dance offerings. As the footprints show, the Dancers have "run to the four directions," as they followed the Sun Dance leader, who carries a stick tipped with a scalp. The Sun Dance ceremony is still practiced by most Plains tribes, and to this day the Cheyenne conduct the dance as Making Medicine depicts it here.

CHEYENNE BUFFALO HUNT.
A COMMON RESULT, THROWN

Buffalo were an integral part of Cheyenne life. From the age of 12, Cheyenne boys accompanied hunting expeditions, learning the skills they would rely on to provide food for their people. These young men assumed more and more responsibility until they were allowed to kill their first animal. It was the custom to put blood from the first kill on the hunter's face.

Novice hunters learned that it was best to approach the buffalo from the right side, thus giving ample room to extend the bow with the left arm. The young hunter also learned that a perfect shot—to the heart—would bring a buffalo down quickly. Making Medicine catches the drama and excitement of a high-speed buffalo hunt on horseback. Not concerned with perspective, he stacks the animals to illustrate a herd of buffalo dashing across the open prairie. Four of the five hunters carry their bow cases and quivers strapped to their backs.

Buffalo hunters needed quick and agile horses. The best warriors usually owned a special horse kept exclusively for buffalo hunting. In order to kill a buffalo, the horse and rider must catch up to the herd and move close to the large beasts. But riding at full gallop across open prairie presented many hazards, especially badger and prairie dog holes. In this drawing, a rider lies sprawled in the dirt. A hoof print drawn inside a circle indicates that the horse stepped into a hole and fell. The lines streaming from the hole are the dirt and dust thrown up by the fallen horse.

Cheyenne Buffalo Hunt.   A common result, thrown.

DISSECTING THE BUFFALO

Making Medicine depicts one aspect of the communal
buffalo hunt, a ritual characterized by strict rules and
protocols. Once an animal was killed, the hunters gutted and
skinned it. At the upper left, two men who have tethered
their horses to a tree are working on the buffalo carcass.
They have laid out the animal's hide, which will be taken
back to camp for tanning. They are cutting the animal into
parts that can be transported more easily on horseback.
Making Medicine shows the men using large knives.
One of them skins the head of the buffalo, which is lying
on its stomach. Considerable chopping and cutting will be
necessary to complete the job.

A third hunter sits on horseback and watches the others.
He casually smokes his pipe, perhaps offering a prayer of
thanks for a successful hunt. Since he is sitting on a folded
buffalo hide, we assume that he has finished skinning and
dissecting another buffalo and that it has already been taken
back to camp.

Dissecting the Buffalo

"A little game"

"Hand" or "Stick" games are a form of entertainment still popular among Indian peoples, and traditionally offered tribal members a chance to socialize. The game pits two teams against each other. One is the "guessing" team; the other is the "hiding" team. Each team holds a specified number of "counters," or tally sticks, which are used for keeping score. The hiding team conceals small game pieces, or "bones," while the opposing team tries to guess which player is holding a bone in his hand. If the guessing team makes a wrong choice, the team gives up a counter; if it makes a correct choice, the team wins one of the counters. When all the counters are won by the opposing team, it becomes the "hiding" team. The object of the game is for one team to collect all of the counters.

Hand-game songs contribute to the excitement of the games, which are often played for high stakes. As the hiding team passes the bones among its players, other members of the team sing songs that are intended to confuse and fool the guessing team. In this drawing, two members of the guessing team are pointing to the hand of the opposing team member they think holds the bone, while another member of the hiding team reveals that he is actually holding it.

SOME FUN WITH A BUFFALO

In an act of sheer bravado, a young man attempts to ride
a buffalo. Although a highly unusual and remarkable feat,
stories of such attempts exist in the oral history of the
Cheyenne. It is reported, for example, that around 1870
a man named Big Ribs jumped from his galloping horse
onto the back of a running buffalo, stabbed it with his knife,
and then leaped from the buffalo to the ground without
being harmed.

Making Medicine depicts a similar act in this drawing.
Two hunters have managed to loop a rope around a buffalo's
head and are attempting to slow it down, while their
companion rides it like a bucking bronco. Making Medicine
captures the determined expression of the rider and clearly
illustrates the effort the men are making as they cling to the
rope. Knowing the situation is dangerous, one hunter has
sought safety in a tree, and another one is joining him.
Making Medicine has drawn a light wavy line from the
mouth of the hunter in the tree to the buffalo rider, an
indication he is yelling encouragement. Another wavy line
can be seen going from the hunter standing in the lower
portion of the drawing to the man running towards the tree.

Many wooded hills rise from the prairie in the drawing
indicating that the event took place near the foothills in
Cheyenne country.

Some fun with a Buffalo.

On the Canadian above Adobe Walls

The Red Water, or the South Canadian River, was a favorite hunting area for the Cheyenne because of its plentiful game. Prior to the arrival of white settlers, Cheyenne hunters regularly visited the upper reaches of the river. Once a trading post, named Adobe Walls, was established there in the 1840s, hunting became more difficult. The post had been built to encourage trade with the Comanche and Kiowa, but was soon abandoned when the tribes ignored it. In 1874, a new trading post—also named Adobe Walls—was built about one mile upstream. The new post served as a center for white hunters interested in buffalo. Five tribes—the Comanche, Kiowa, Arapaho, Prairie Apache, and the Cheyenne—formed an alliance to drive the hunters from their country and save the buffalo, and while the tribes' attack on Adobe Walls failed, it inspired the massive retaliation by the federal government that led to the Fort Marion experience.

In this drawing Making Medicine illustrates the abundant wildlife found along the river. Two hunters stalk game. Tracks that run atop the hills show the path followed by the turkey hunter. Another hunter carefully approaches a group of unsuspecting buffalo. The hunters have tethered their horses to a tree where the two ridge lines meet. With the two wavy lines of hills that meet at lower right, Making Medicine alerts the viewer that the hunters are in a secluded valley.

OSAGE DANCE

Dancing remains a vital part of Plains Indian life. An art form that provides social and celebratory, as well spiritual expression, traditional dancing is a manifestation of ethnic identity. Most dances today are pan-Indian. Historically, when peoples of different tribes came in contact, they borrowed or adopted cultural attributes from one another. Music and dance were no exception. In this drawing, Making Medicine shows Cheyenne villagers watching Osage visitors performing a dance. The Osage can be identified by their shaved heads and scalp locks, usually adorned with a single eagle feather. The dancers may have come to trade with the Cheyenne and are expressing their gratitude at the generosity of their hosts by entertaining them with this vigorous and colorful dance. It is often called a war dance because of the weapons brandished by the dancers.

The prisoners at Fort Marion performed the "Osage dance" on the two occasions Capt. Pratt permitted them to hold dances. Pratt, who misnamed it the "Omaha Dance" in his memoirs, claimed the dance—"celebrated and used throughout the central West by all the Indians—was the most spectacular because of its very remarkable posing and posturing."

Osage Dance

Big Dance at Cheyenne Agency
1873

BIG DANCE AT CHEYENNE AGENCY 1873

A PLAY UPON CURIOSITY

Dances, which offer a chance to renew old friendships, visit with relatives, and rejuvenate cultural traditions, have long been a part of Native American culture. Men and women put on their finest clothes for these occasions. The outfits worn by men and women often indicated their membership in tribal societies. As they stood or sat around the dance arbor, participants often covered themselves with a blanket, removing it when they stepped into the circle to dance revealing stunning outfits which required many hours of painstaking labor to prepare. Many were made of tanned skins and decorated with beads, dentalium shells, and porcupine quills. Umbrellas were prominently displayed— they were not only useful for keeping cool on hot sunny days, but Indians also considered them stylish.

In this drawing, people are still arriving at the dance area from their camp, while others wait for the dance to begin. On one side of the dance arbor, singers hold their hand drums, while across from them, in a wooden reviewing stand, a number of white visitors gather. The white women appear to be fascinated by the colorful spectacle, as they look around and point out their favorite dancers.

Leaving tracks, a Cheyenne hunter stalks a small group of pronghorn antelope walking along a river. He has already shot and killed one of the animals, which lies on the ground bleeding from its mouth and from the bullet wound. The hunter, who is well hidden in the brush behind a row of hills, attracts the attention of five pronghorn—three bucks and two does—who have been slowly coming closer to him. Pronghorns are by nature curious animals, a trait which makes them easy prey for a hunter armed with a rifle. When the Cheyenne hunter feels the herd is close enough for a clean shot, he steadies his rifle on two crossed sticks and takes careful aim. He pulls the trigger and hits the nearest buck with a perfect shot in the chest.

A play upon curiosity

Moving

Cheyenne were dependent upon the wandering herds of buffalo for their livelihood and were adapted to moving entire villages efficiently and quickly. Most personal belongings, prepared foods, and other loose items were packed into rawhide containers known as parfleches and attached to a travois, a basic carrier made from a pair of crossed tepee poles dragged by a horse. When it was time to move camp, travois were constructed, loaded, and moved with the herd of horses. Each family owned a pack of dogs as well as several horses. Villages on the move were colorful, noisy, and dusty.

Making Medicine shows two women moving their horses and camp gear. Two mules carry brightly painted parfleches and drag tepee poles. One set of poles has cross straps indicating it is a travois. The women carry whips and ride on each side of the small herd as they attempt to keep the animals together and headed in the same direction. One woman wears a blue wool dress decorated with elk ivories which run from arm to arm and across her chest. Just two teeth in the jaw of the elk are considered to be ivories, which were highly valued trade items; one hundred would pay for a good horse. Only a woman married to an outstanding hunter would possess a dress like this one, embellished with dozens of elk ivories.

CHEYENNE LODGE.
VISITORS TO TALK UP A DANCE

At the time of his capture and imprisonment, Making Medicine was a member of the honored Bowstring Society, a hundred-year-old military society. Like other military societies, the Bowstrings held meetings similar to the one shown here. Many society members are in attendance. Society lances—as distinctive as a knight's coat of arms— are stuck into the ground in front of the tepee. Two members have tied their horses to their lances. Two other members, still holding their lances, wait to participate in the meeting. The warrior on the right with his back turned to the viewer displays his German silver hairplates, a valuable adornment that was tied to the hair and extended to the ground.

Making Medicine has used an unusual artistic convention to show that the meeting is being held under a large cover or awning. Instead of drawing a line over the warriors, he has flipped the rectangular cover on its side. Another row of lances protrudes above the cover on the other side, indicating that the society meeting is well-attended.

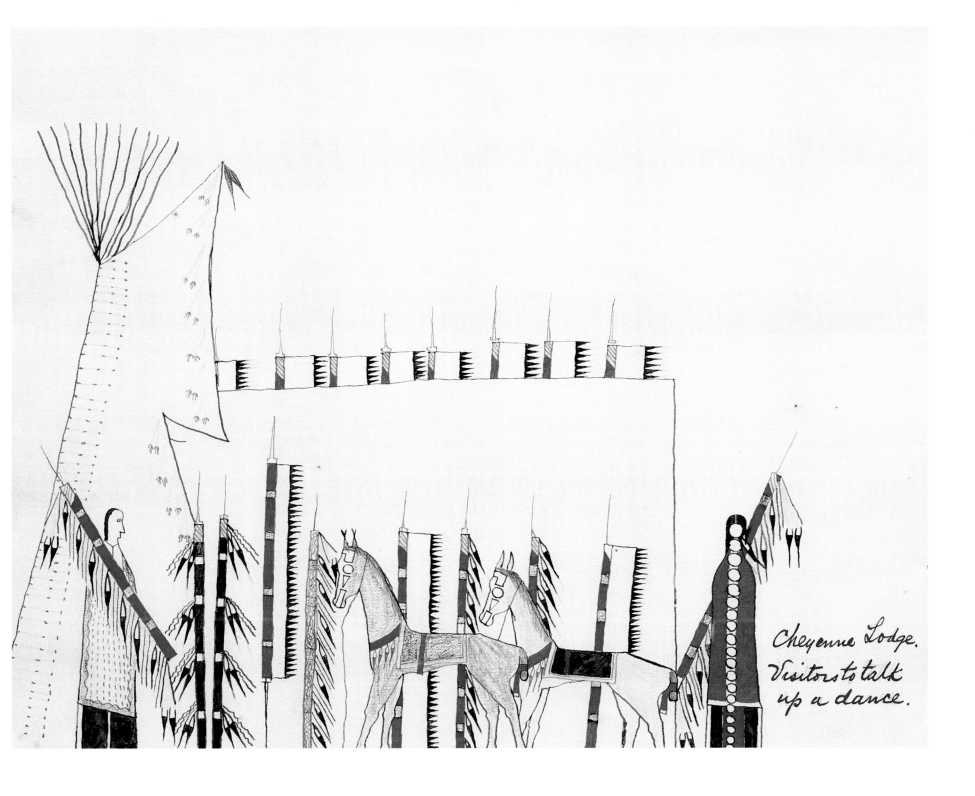

Cheyenne Lodge.
Visitors to talk
up a dance.

Gambling

GAMBLING

Plains Indians loved to gamble. Excitement increased when personal skills were involved, as in this archery match. Two groups of men have selected their best marksman to represent them in the contest. The target is an arrow stuck into the ground. Each archer has a predetermined number of arrows to shoot. The winner is the archer whose arrows come closest to the target. Each group designates a member to officiate. Standing near the target, he ensures that the other team follows the rules, and he shouts instructions to his archer, advising him of the accuracy of each shot. Both groups of warriors wear their finest regalia. It is clearly a hot summer day. Several men shield themselves from the bright sun with colorful umbrellas, which, like blankets, were a popular trade item. Two warriors cool themselves with fans made from eagle feathers.

Running down Antelope

RUNNING DOWN ANTELOPE

Four mounted hunters pursue two buck pronghorn antelopes. One animal is already dead; its body is outstretched with blood coming from its nose and mouth. The horse above the dead pronghorn turns to look at it while riding past at full gallop. The animal still on its feet has already been hit with one arrow and is about to be struck by another from a hunter in close pursuit.

Four of the five hunters are carrying bow cases and quivers made from mountain lion skins. The paws, which can be seen dangling off the straps and bow cases, were left attached to the hides when the mountain lions were skinned. Mountain lions were known to be skilled hunters—they caught their prey through stealth and then dispatched it quickly and efficiently. By making his quiver and bow case from a mountain lion skin, the Indian hunter hoped the animal's hunting skills would pass to him. When a noted hunter died, his skin quiver and bow case were not buried with him. Instead, they were given to a relative or close friend in an effort to transfer his hunting prowess.

WAITING FOR THE BUFFALO

In this two-page drawing, Cheyenne hunters await a small herd of thirsty buffalo as the animals cautiously approach a small stream. The buffalo are clearly nervous. Several lift their noses to catch any strange smells. They sense that everything is not as it should be.

The hunters, aware that the buffalo smell something, try to be as silent as possible. One hunter wears an otterskin turban decorated with small silver disks. He also has his braids wrapped in cloth, indicated by the black and white triangles draped down his chest. He is a person of distinction.

The tracks of the hunters indicate a cautious approach to their hiding places in the brush and embankments along the stream. One hunter signals his laggard companion to hurry, because the buffalo are almost within range of the guns. Each hunter carries a powerful rifle—he can be confident of killing a buffalo even from a considerable distance. Two of the marksmen carry crossed sticks which they will use to steady their rifles as they take aim.

Waiting for the Buffalo.

Scenes in the life of an Indian
Prisoner, by Zotom (Biter), Kiowa Warrior,
"Fort Marion, Fla,
Mch, 1877

Kiowa Camp, Elk Cr, Witchita Mts 1873

KIOWA CAMP, ELK CR. WICHITA MTS 1873

Zotom opens his section of the ledger book with drawings that establish him as part of two worlds, the Indian world and the white world. The first drawing shows a Kiowa camp along a timbered creek on a grassy meadow nestled in the Wichita Mountains, the heartland of his Kiowa people. On the following page is a drawing of Fort Sill, the place where the world, as he knew it, ended.

The number of painted tepees in the camp suggests the presence of a large number of prominent tribal leaders. Only men of stature and wealth would decorate their homes in such an elaborate manner, and in a typical Kiowa camp, fewer than one in five tepee covers were painted in such a dramatic fashion. Tepee designs were family property, like a medieval coat of arms, and were handed down from generation to generation. In a remarkable coincidence, Zotom was later hired by the Smithsonian Institution to paint the covers of model tepees in an effort to preserve these distinctive heraldic designs before they were lost to memory.

It is likely that Zotom is depicting a council meeting— many people in the camp circle, including several men on horses, wear full eagle-feather warbonnets. An American flag, also visible, possibly indicates that the council members are listening to a message from the Kiowa Indian agent or another government representative urging them to give up their nomadic ways and return to the reservation.

FORT SILL, INDIAN TERRITORY

Named for Joshua Sill, a West Point classmate of Gen. Phillip Sheridan, Fort Sill was established in 1869. Located near the foot of the Wichita Mountains at the junction of Cache and Medicine Bluff creeks in what is now Oklahoma, Fort Sill was an important outpost in the wars against the southern Plains Indians. Between 1870 and 1878, it also served as the agency for the Comanche and Kiowa Indians. The fort held bitter memories for Zotom; it was here that he was first imprisoned before being sent east in chains.

Fort Sill, Ind. Territory

ALMOST A BATTLE, SWEET WATER CR. I.T. 1871

In the summer of 1870, Kicking Bird's village left the reservation in violation of the Medicine Lodge Treaty. Col. Benjamin H. Grierson and two companies of the Tenth Cavalry found the Indians along the banks of Sweet Water Creek, which formed the western boundary of the Kiowa reservation. According to Capt. Pratt, the cavalry saw warriors on a large rise of ground forming a line of battle at their front. "[We] continued our advance. The Indians were massed, and as we came nearer we discovered, with our glasses, that they had on their war bonnets and were evidently inviting a contest." Grierson held his troops in check and approached the Indians at a slow walk until only a half mile separated the two forces. At that moment a warrior carrying a white flag rode out to meet the troops. Pratt and an interpreter met the warrior who said Kicking Bird wanted to talk, not fight. After meeting with Grierson, Kicking Bird signaled his warriors, who then disappeared behind the surrounding hills. As it was late in the day, Grierson decided to spend the night. The following morning the troops discovered that Kicking Bird's entire village had been camped outside the reservation boundaries and that the threatening movements of his warriors had merely been a diversion to give the women and children time to take down the tepees and return to the reservation.

Zotom shows Pratt, the interpreter, and white flag carrier in front of the advancing troops as warriors watch from nearby slopes.

Almost a battle, Sweet Water Cr. I.T. 1871

Kiowas under "Big Bow" Surrendering. Feby 1875.

KIOWA UNDER "BIG BOW"
SURRENDERING. FEB 1875

The surrender of Big Bow, chief of Zotom's village, took place in the Wichita Mountains about 40 miles west of Fort Sill and was negotiated by the commandant of the Fort and tribal leaders Napawat and Kicking Bird. In February 1875, Capt. Pratt set out from Fort Sill accompanied by Kicking Bird, Napawat, 16 Kiowa scouts, 4 black teamsters, and a white interpreter.

Zotom depicts Pratt, Kicking Bird, Napawat, and several scouts meeting with Big Bow's representatives, who carry a flag of truce.

In exchange for his surrender, Big Bow was promised immunity from punishment. Pratt felt the chief should have been executed, not pardoned, and was later shocked to learn that the Army had hired Big Bow as a scout. "I am informed from Fort Sill that the Kiowa chief, Big Bow, the leader of the Howard's Well massacre, the hero of numerous other atrocities, and the peer of any here in bad acts, whose offenses were condoned for special services last winter, is [now] a government enlisted scout at the cantonment on the North Fork of Red River," an outraged Pratt wrote to the Adjutant General in July 1875. "Many of the young Kiowas imprisoned here justly attribute their unfortunate position to his bad influences, and sensibly contrast their situation with his."

IN CAMP, NIGHT AFTER SURRENDER

Following Big Bow's surrender, Capt. Pratt and his scouts collected weapons; compiled a census of the village taking the names of the men; counted tepees, horses, and mules; and then issued rations to each family. Pleased to have resolved the crisis without bloodshed, the Kiowas invited Pratt to a dance held at Big Bow's tepee. Pratt sat on a blanket to one side of the fire; a small open area opposite served as the dance floor. The festivities began awkwardly. No one seemed willing to dance. At last a young man carrying a large butcher knife stepped forward, danced briefly, and then stepped onto Pratt's blanket and leaned forward as if to stab him. Instead, he reached behind Pratt, wrestled briefly with a young man, and then returned to the dance area clutching a blanket. To the delight of the excited crowd, he slashed it with his knife. "This," Pratt was relieved to see, "inspired the whole party with extraordinary enthusiasm and without delay other young men rose and danced—two, three, four at a time, and then women and children."

Not until months later did Pratt learn that the dancer was Zotom, and that Big Bow had ordered him to shame another young man who had refused to start the dance. It was his blanket that Zotom destroyed. Zotom's drawing shows the crowd assembled in front of Big Bow's large tepee. Everyone, including Pratt, watches Zotom who is in the center of the scene. "The incidents of that dance," Pratt later wrote, "are among the most vivid in my memory."

In camp, night after surrender.

Meeting the troops near "Fort Sill.

MEETING THE TROOPS NEAR FORT SILL

The march to Fort Sill took two days. In this drawing Zotom
shows Big Bow's villagers proceeding in a long column led by
Pratt's army wagons. To mark the event with appropriate
military ceremony—and perhaps to guard against a last
moment change of heart on the part of Big Bow or some of
his warriors—two companies of cavalry meet the caravan to
escort Pratt and the prisoners into Fort Sill. The rendezvous
occurred at Mount Scott, about nine miles to the northwest.

Fort Sill was the Comanche and Kiowa Indian agency. Zotom was doubtless well acquainted with the cavalry fort and its environs, and he might well have been one of the raiders led by Chief White Horse, who embarrassed the garrison while the fort was being constructed by taking its herd of 73 mules. The focal point of Zotom's drawing is the fort's ceremonial center: the parade and drill ground with its tall flagpole. The impressive white building on the left is the hospital. Surrounding the vast parade ground are officer's quarters, barracks, and administrative buildings. While a small group of Indians watch, an officer drills his cavalry troop.

Arrival at Ft Sill.

Selecting the men for imprisonment

IN CAMP SECOND NIGHT OUT

The Army took every precaution to prevent an escape or
rescue attempt. Guarded by two troops of the Fourth Cavalry,
the Indians occupied eight wagons in the center of a large
train. They sat on straw bedding in two rows; each was
shackled with ankle irons, and a chain down the center of
wagon passed between their legs joining them together.
Additional wagons carried tents for the soldiers, bedding,
rations, feed for the horses and mules, and other camp gear.
At night, the prisoners slept between two Army wagons. To
prevent the men's escape, five sections of chain were joined
together "making a continuous chain on which the prisoners
were strung, half on one side and half on the other, the ends
being padlocked to the wagons." In this drawing, Zotom
provides a snapshot of the camp at dusk. The Army tents are
up. Most of the soldiers lounge in front of their tents, or are
already inside them for the night. The prisoners sit in the
center of the large square formed by the wagons and the
tents. The guards may have feared a dramatic rescue
attempt, but none occurred.

CAMP ON "THE BLUE"

The 165-mile wagon trip to Caddo, the nearest railroad
junction, took eight days. Capt. Pratt did his best to make
things bearable for his prisoners. "During each day," he later
wrote, "there were halts during which the prisoners were let
out of the wagons, and we camped by running water each
night, when the prisoners, under guard, went to convenient
places where they could perform such cleansing of
themselves as they were able to under the limitations of
their shackles." In this drawing Zotom presents one of the
more pleasant campsites. It was the last night on the trail,
and camp was made alongside the wagon road at the
Blue River crossing. Caddo was less than 20 miles away.
Some of the prisoners are in the water, others relax along
the riverbank. A few have already bedded down for the
night in the camp circle.

Camp on "The Blue"

Arrival at Caddoe, I.T.

On April 30, the caravan reached the railroad junction at Caddo, Indian Territory. Here the prisoners boarded a train waiting to speed them eastward towards Fort Marion. Zotom depicts the train, a crowd of spectators at the platform, and in the background, the men approaching in their wagons. For all of the prisoners except Lone Wolf, a Kiowa chief who had been a delegate from his tribe to Washington, D.C., in 1863, this was to be their first train ride. It also marked the beginning of an astounding array of new experiences that must have been both exhilarating and terrifying. The prisoners's reactions were probably similar to those of other Indians making their first visit to urban areas. For them, steamboats were "fire boats"; railroad tracks were the "iron road"; and locomotives were either "fast wagons," "iron horses," "fire horses," or "puffing wagons." One Indian, after his first train ride, told his friends that the train was "a fast wagon" pulled by a large black horse whose belly almost touched the ground. The horse carried a large bell, and whenever he stopped to rest, he would be puffing so hard that his bell would ring.

Established on the west bank of the Missouri River in 1827, Fort Leavenworth was the first stop on the journey east for Capt. Pratt and his prisoners.

For three days, hundreds of people jammed the station, waiting for the Missouri Pacific train believed to be carrying the prisoners. When the Indians finally arrived on May 8, the Fort Leavenworth *Daily Times* reported that: "The vociferous greeting which [the crowd] extended to the Indians was lusty enough to have suited the most fastidious." The train consisted of five coaches. "The prisoners, shackled, numbering 74, were confined in two cars, with guards on the front and rear platforms, while the two rear cars were filled with the officers and soldiers escorting the party." According to the reporter, "The wild men of the plains presented a sorry sight to the beholder as they emerged from the cars, with their long, shaggy, unkempt hair, careworn faces and dirty, variegated blankets. They were placed in the wagons, ten to each vehicle, while two sick ones…were lifted into an uncovered ambulance. Thus, with soldiers to the left, right, front, and behind them, they were conveyed to the military guard house, where they are to be confined until they are brought out either for court-martial or consignment to Florida. … It is believed that…some of them will yet stretch hemp."

In documenting their 10-day stay at Fort Leavenworth, Zotom chose to record a flag ceremony with an honor guard and a drum and bugle corps.

At "Ft Leavenworth

St Louis Bridge

ST. LOUIS BRIDGE

Zotom's artistic skills are especially evident in his rendering of buildings and other structures which he painted with almost photographic fidelity. One shows a trestle bridge over the Missouri River which linked St. Louis by rail with its sister city, St. Charles, and points west. Completed in 1871, it was the first railroad bridge over the Missouri and boasted the longest main spans in the United States. Once across the bridge, the track curved sharply on its route into St. Louis and provided passengers a clear view of the architectural marvel they had just crossed. This explains why Zotom was able to later make this remarkable drawing, which compares well to the stereoscopic view of the St. Charles Bridge above.

ARRIVAL AT INDIANAPOLIS

On May 18, the prisoners reached Indianapolis, Indiana, where
Capt. Pratt was joined by his family, and by George L. Fox, the
Comanche interpreter. Fox was a welcome addition to the
company, and he enabled Pratt to communicate with the
Comanche and Kiowa prisoners with more than hand gestures.

According to the story in the Indianapolis *Daily Sentinel*
headlined "BAD INDIANS," a large crowd had gathered at the
station to catch a glimpse of the prisoners who were expected
on the Jefferson Road's evening train. The cars carrying the
Indians were switched to a siding until a southbound train
arrived, and the prisoners were promptly surrounded by a large
and curious throng. "Some of the noble red men were disposed
to be retiring, and shut down their windows and screens,
reserving only a small aperture through which they gazed upon
the crowd," the newspaper reported. "Others were very affable,
shaking hands with whoever tendered this token of amity, and
venturing upon the treacherous sea of the English language to
the uttermost extent of their vocabularies. Several ladies passed
through the cars and were received with great urbanity by the
inmates, who all shook hands with them. ... The Indians were
dressed more or less in army uniforms, and their long hair was
ornamented with all sorts of barbaric splendor. ... Taken all
together, the prisoners made a curious spectacle as well as a
puzzling problem for the government. Perhaps the idea of the
powers that be is that a trip over the southern railroads will
solve the question of what is to be done with them without
further trouble to themselves."

Arrival at Indianapolis.

Leaving "Lean Bear" at Nashville

In his pictorial diary of the journey to Fort Marion, Zotom documented its two most tragic episodes—the attempted suicide of Lean Bear, and the death of Gray Beard. Zotom is known to have drawn several versions of these scenes which differ only slightly from one another in perspective, angle of presentation, and detail. Here, the train idles on the track at the Nashville railway station while a large group of uniformed men surround the gravely wounded Lean Bear and the two soldiers he stabbed.

Capt. Pratt informed Washington of Lean Bear's suicide attempt with the following wire: "May 19, 1875. Just as we arrived at Nashville, Lean Bear, one of the Cheyenne Prisoners, who had become crazed by the excitement of the trip, covering himself with his blanket stabbed himself twice in the neck with a small pocket knife and then stabbed two of the guard who were issuing rations—Corporal Allen twice in the back severe and Pvt. Henderson once in the breast slight. I left Lt. Rousseau with the Indian and two wounded men at Nashville. The Indian will die. Lt. Rousseau follows by next train."

Rousseau later informed Pratt that the corporal's wounds were not as severe as first believed, and that Lean Bear was still alive, but near death. Lean Bear made an unexpected recovery, however, and rejoined the prisoners at Fort Marion, where he refused to eat or talk, even to his son, who was also a prisoner. The death he so desperately wanted eluded him until the morning of July 24, 1875.

The prisoners reached Macon, Georgia, on May 20, having ridden trains for three days. They were met by a respectful and sympathetic reporter for *The Telegraph and Messenger,* who wrote a lengthy story based on interviews with the guards, Capt. Pratt, and a man of Cheyenne-Mexican heritage named Rafael Romero, whom reporters called Romeo. The Indians remained in Macon for about an hour and drew a large crowd of curiosity seekers.

"The fate of these men is pitiful," the reporter noted. "They have been told they are going to a new reservation where they will be dealt with by honest agents, but it is probable they will never be set at liberty again. They will be scorched by a Florida sun and preyed upon by malaria of a clime to which they are wholly unaccustomed and they will soon perish. They have been compelled to yield to the surge of white men which has swept them from the rising to the setting sun, and which, in a few years more will leave not a man to tell the world that such a race of human beings ever existed. Their traditions will be forgotten, or only dimly remembered, through the records of partial history. …
No sadder history of the destruction of a race of people has ever been written."

These observations, written more than a century ago, were remarkably prescient. Little could this reporter have realized that among the prisoners whose fate he was lamenting were two men—Zotom and Making Medicine— who would record these traditions for future generations.

A rest at Macon

Killing of "Grey Beard" near Baldwin

KILLING OF "GREY BEARD" NEAR BALDWIN

Two days after Lean Bear attempted suicide, Chief Gray Beard tried to escape by jumping from a train window. The news immediately went up the chain of command, and a telegram reached the Adjutant General in Washington, D.C., that afternoon: "May 21, 1875. Gray Beard, Cheyenne Chief, jumped out of a car window at three O'clock this morning near Houston, Fla. The train backed up and we found him. He attempted to run away and was shot by the Sergeant of the Guard and died in two hours. Body left at Baldwin, Fla."

According to Capt. Pratt's report, "One of the young Cheyennes wanted me to tie Gray Beard's hands and fasten him to a seat on the evening before he jumped from the car, but…[his] behavior and talk to me through the Interpreter and the Interpreter's confidence made me believe that was unnecessary. After the train had backed up and we had searched the ground where he had jumped from the car without finding him…Gray Beard jumped up from bushes near the rear end of the train and started down the track. He was discovered by the Sergeant and his jumps and speed were such as to lead the Sergeant to think he had gotten his shackles off and the Sergeant fired one shot which took effect in the left side of the chest and came out nearly opposite."

Before he died, Gray Beard gave his friend, Minimic, a message for his wife and daughter. According to the interpreter, Gray Beard told his companions he had wanted to die from the moment he had been placed in chains and taken away. Pratt later assured his superiors that the other Indians were not unduly upset by these two incidents. "They say if they were foolish enough to kill themselves it was their business." Perhaps that was true, but Zotom documented the killing, ensuring that Gray Beard would not be forgotten.

FROM CARS TO STEAMER AT JACKSONVILLE FLA.

Leaving Gray Beard's body at Baldwin, the party continued to Jacksonville, Florida. There the prisoners encountered still another of the white man's wonders, a steamboat, which carried them on the St. John's River to the town of Tocoi, Florida, where they transferred to the Tocoi and St. Augustine Railroad for the short ride to their final destination, Fort Marion.

"The old Spanish fort at St. Augustine," announced a Jacksonville newspaper, "is to be converted into a military prison, for the reception of a number of rebellious Indians, from the Western reservations, now in custody of the U.S. Army. The cells formerly occupied by the Seminole chiefs, Osceola and Tiger Tail, have been put in order, and others are undergoing repairs for the accommodation of the red men of the forest. These are the gentlemen General Miles has been entertaining for the past week, at Fort Leavenworth."

From Cars to Steamer at Jacksonville Fla.

Arrival at St. Augustine May 21st 1875

ARRIVAL AT ST. AUGUSTINE MAY 21ST 1875

A steamboat carried the prisoners from Jacksonville, Florida, up the St. John's River to Tocoi Landing, where they boarded a train for the final 20 miles of their cross-country journey to the East Coast. Zotom shows the prisoners in the carts that transported them from the St. Augustine train station to Fort Marion, the former Spanish fortress on the Atlantic shore. Once inside, the only link to the world the prisoners had left behind was Capt. Pratt, the Army officer who escorted them to Florida. The trip must have both terrified and excited the Indians who had left their world and entered one entirely new and unknown to them. Little wonder then, as Pratt later remarked, "the events of the trip so vividly impressed the Indians that some of them, with artistic ability, drew pictures of its features and sold them to visitors throughout their imprisonment."

MELANCHOLY PROSPECT FROM FT MARION, DAY OF ARRIVAL

In one of Zotom's most haunting drawings, Indians, watched by two armed guards and still in ankle chains, stare out at the sea, the horizon broken only by two lighthouses and a steamboat reminiscent of the vessel that carried them from Jacksonville. Few could have anticipated what awaited them, but once they crossed the moat and entered Fort Marion there was no misunderstanding. For the next three years, home for these free-spirited nomads was a windowless pen with walls 20 feet high.

Fort Marion, formerly named the Castillo de San Marcos, the oldest masonry fort in the United States, is essentially a hollow square with diamond-shaped bastions at each corner (above). The fort casements, which served as cells, have no outside openings other than two barred windows that face the hundred-foot-square interior court and narrow ventilation slots near the top of the 18-foot high ceilings. Each casement also had a heavy steel door locked by a bolt and padlock. Access to the terreplein, the broad platform behind the parapet, was restricted to keep the Indians from escaping. The fort's entrance was across a drawbridge and through a wide hall secured by two massive pitch-pine doors. "The only outlook besides the sky the prisoners could have," according to Capt. Pratt, "was by going to the terreplein under charge of the guard, which was done several times each day. Otherwise they were confined to the court below and the casements in which they slept. Plank floors had been put into several of these to make them more sanitary. The prisoners slept on the floors."

Melancholy prospect from "Ft Marion, day after arrival.

Catching Sharks on the Beach — July & Aug. 1875

CATCHING SHARKS ON THE BEACH—
JULY & AUG. 1875

The Indian prisoners greatly enjoyed fishing for sharks. A deep channel along north beach at the entrance to St. Augustine harbor offered them the best access to the sharks, which the Indians called "water buffaloes." To catch a shark, one end of a long, heavy line was tied to a stake on shore; the other end, attached to a length of chain and iron hook baited with ten pounds of fresh fish or beef, was taken by rowboat and dropped into the channel. "Sometimes," Capt. Pratt wrote, "the shark was the stronger in the tug of war and would successfully pull against the Indians until all the line was paid out and only the fastening at the shore end stopped him. It was great sport for the 20 or more Indians who whooped and tugged and pulled until the shark surrendered." Their best one-day catch was five sharks including one that weighed an estimated 1,200 pounds.

A Buffalo Chase. Dec 1875

Public pressure to have the Indians put on a traditional dance caused Capt. Pratt to agree to one performance. A local citizen donated a bull for the occasion, and the dance included a simulated "buffalo" hunt as well. People talked of little else, wrote one visitor, "in anticipation of witnessing the realities, in miniature, connected with a buffalo-chase on the prairies." Long before the 3 p.m. starting time, throngs of richly dressed ladies escorted by gentlemen sporting "New-York style mustaches" and youngsters "of all sizes and colors" had assembled on the grounds outside the fort where they saw four "painted, gaily-dressed, full-rigged Indians" put on a spectacular equestrian demonstration that included firing arrows at a shed some 200 yards distant while riding at full gallop. The horsemen then turned their attention to the bull, but it was either too tame or too frightened to run. According to the visitor, "he shook his head once or twice, and started as though he might create a sensation, but would not keep far enough ahead for the hunters to make anything like a good charge on him. Finally an arrow, sped from the bow of White Horse, pierced his vitals to the depth of four or five inches, killing him instantly." The bull was then dragged into the fort, where it was quickly butchered and the meat tossed into boiling kettles of water. Those Indians not involved in preparing the feast entertained the visitors with drumming and dancing. Then, after enjoying a hearty meal, the entire company capped the day with a "grand war dance" around a blazing bonfire in the center of the prison courtyard.

A DANCE IN THE FORT. 1875

The first dance proved so popular that Capt. Pratt consented to another, with the understanding that it would be the last and that all monies raised would support the education of the prisoners. Sponsored by the St. Augustine Yacht Club, the "Indian Sports and War Dance" featured an afternoon of arrow throwing and an archery competition, followed by an evening of dances around a blazing bonfire. Reserved seats in the courtyard were 50 cents; open seating on the ramparts was available for 25 cents.

According to Pratt, it "was perhaps as picturesque and thrilling a performance as any of its kind ever produced on the continent." The Indians made drums, chose a chorus of singers, and selected their best dancers who painted their bodies "impressively." The visitors loved the entire evening, but they were thrilled by the "Osage War Dance" with its "remarkable posing and posturing," which Zotom depicts here.

This event ended the theatrical career of the Fort Marion prisoners because, as Pratt explained, such performances did not promote their advancement. "I had the consciousness, however, forever after that, that had I been so minded I could have handled the Indians more wisely and out 'Buffalo Billed' Mr. Cody in his line."

A dance in the Fort. 1875

Camp on the Beach Sept & Oct, 1875

As fears of an attempted escape lessened, the Indians were issued tents and permitted to camp on nearby beaches. During these outings which sometimes lasted for a week, Indians searched for materials to make crafts they later sold to tourists. These crafts included bows and arrows and sea shells and sea beans that they polished and decorated.

The beach shown here, on the ocean side of Anastasia Island, the barrier island between the fort and the Atlantic Ocean, stretched for 16 miles, and was so solid at low tide that it made an ideal track for footraces and other sports. On one occasion two of the best long-distance runners raced each other for a distance of 30 miles. According to Capt. Pratt, "these contests were usually intertribal, which was a great stimulation."

A SAIL

The prisoners readily adapted to life by the sea. They
especially enjoyed beachcombing and the sailing excursions
which Capt. Pratt arranged by chartering local vessels.
Eventually, the prisoners obtained two small sailboats when
a schooner from Maine foundered on a nearby beach. At first
the ship's captain tried to save his vessel by hiring the
Indians to pull it off the beach, but each tide only buried it
deeper in the sand. Pratt bought the schooner and its two
yawls, which he later rigged with sails. After learning to sail
and to row these vessels, some of the prisoners began taking
tourists for boat rides. These, Pratt claimed, "became
something of a favorite feature in the local services of that
kind to visitors."

DRILL

Zotom documented an important part of the Fort Marion experience, the transition of the Indians from prisoners to soldiers. Capt. Pratt introduced a number of non-regulation innovations, but none seemed riskier than freeing the prisoners from their chains and treating them as Army recruits instead of convicts. Forming a squad of 50 or so soldiers commanded by their own sergeants and corporals (above), the Indians were issued old guns, and allowed to police themselves. Pratt overcame Army objections by promising to resign his commission if the experiment failed.

The Indians learned to clean and press their uniforms; burnish their brass buttons, buckles, and cap insignia; and shine their shoes. Within a remarkably short time, the former warriors attained an espirit de corps that would have brightened the face of the Army's most hard-hearted drill instructor. Their proudest moment came when Gen. Winfield Scott Hancock, commander of the Department of the East, paid an unexpected visit during drill. The general had been standing unnoticed in a doorway, as the Indians conducted their drill at double time, when someone brought the distinguished visitor to Pratt's attention. He immediately brought the company to a halt facing Hancock, ordered a hand salute, then walked over to the general, and delivered his own salute. Hancock returned Pratt's salute, but never took his eyes off the Indians as he asked: "What troops are these, sir?"

Zotom depicts the Indian soldiers executing the order, "Left Face." They are as precise and erect as any honor guard, and obviously proud soldiers. Capt. Pratt seldom missed an opportunity to bring their accomplishments to the Army's attention. "[I] Have just had a new issue of clothing and a majority of them went voluntarily and paid the barbers for a hair cut," he wrote on May 15, 1876. "They make fine looking soldiers." This sentiment was repeated two months later in a note to Lt. Gen. Phil Sheridan: "There is nothing of note to report regarding these prisoners unless that fact is of itself important. They are simply under good discipline…and are as neat and clean in their dress and persons as the men of a disciplined company."

Pratt's claims were endorsed by Gen. N.G. Davis, Inspector General of the Army, who paid a surprise visit in 1877. "The result of my personal inspection of these Indians and their quarters at this Old Fort, was highly gratifying and satisfactory as to their condition, and progress towards civilized life, and of their fitness and capacity for industrious occupation and self support, if under proper influences and control," Davis reported. "They performed the ordinary routine of garrison duties, with a military regularity and correctness, closely approximating in this respect the execution at our military posts."

Drill

School

HARPERS WEEKLY, MAY 11, 1878. COURTESY HERMAN J. VIOLA

SCHOOL

Education was a cornerstone of the Fort Marion experience. Capt. Pratt considered a knowledge of English essential so that the prisoners could communicate with one another as well as the white community. Pratt, therefore, welcomed teachers who volunteered their time to instruct the Indians. At any given time during the three-year internment, there were from four to six classes in session each weekday (above). At first the older Indians rejected the opportunity to learn English, but eventually several of them joined the class. The primary classroom was the fort chapel. Former abolitionist Harriet Beecher Stowe wrote a glowing testimonial published in the *Christian Union,* April 18, 1877.

When the bell rang for school hours, there came rushing from all quarters dark men "in the United States uniform, neat, compact, trim, with well-brushed boots and nicely kept clothing and books in their hands." For a time, until all the teachers had arrived, the students formed a square around the blackboards. "Large spelling-cards adorned one side of the wall, containing various pictures and object-lessons adapted to the earliest stages of learning. …When they read in concert, when they mastered perfectly the pronunciation of a difficult word, when they gave the right answer to a question, they were evidently delighted. … There was not a listless face, not a wandering eye, in the whole class."

Religious instruction was another cornerstone of the Fort Marion experience. Harriet Beecher Stowe, who owned a home near the fort, was one of the many visitors to the weekly prayer services. The service she attended was conducted by the Reverend Dr. Marsh in the fort chapel, "a little vaulted room. …roughly fitted up with board seats, and the whole of the Indians were there seated together." The Indians sang from little "Moody and Sankey" hymnbooks they carried in their coat pockets. They listened attentively to a homily by Dr. Marsh and then heartfelt comments from five or six of their fellow prisoners. "Such, then," Stowe declared, "has been the result of two years' imprisonment of these Indians in the center of a Christian community, who have cared for them and treated them in the spirit of the Christian religion." Zotom illustrates several visitors seated behind Capt. Pratt, who is speaking to the prisoners. Next to him is George Fox, the Comanche interpreter. According to Bishop Whipple, who frequently preached to the prisoners, Fox was so proficient in sign language that his translation of the "story of Joseph and his brethren…was understood by all the prisoners of [the] four different tribes."

Service

Capt. Pratt & Mr Fox.

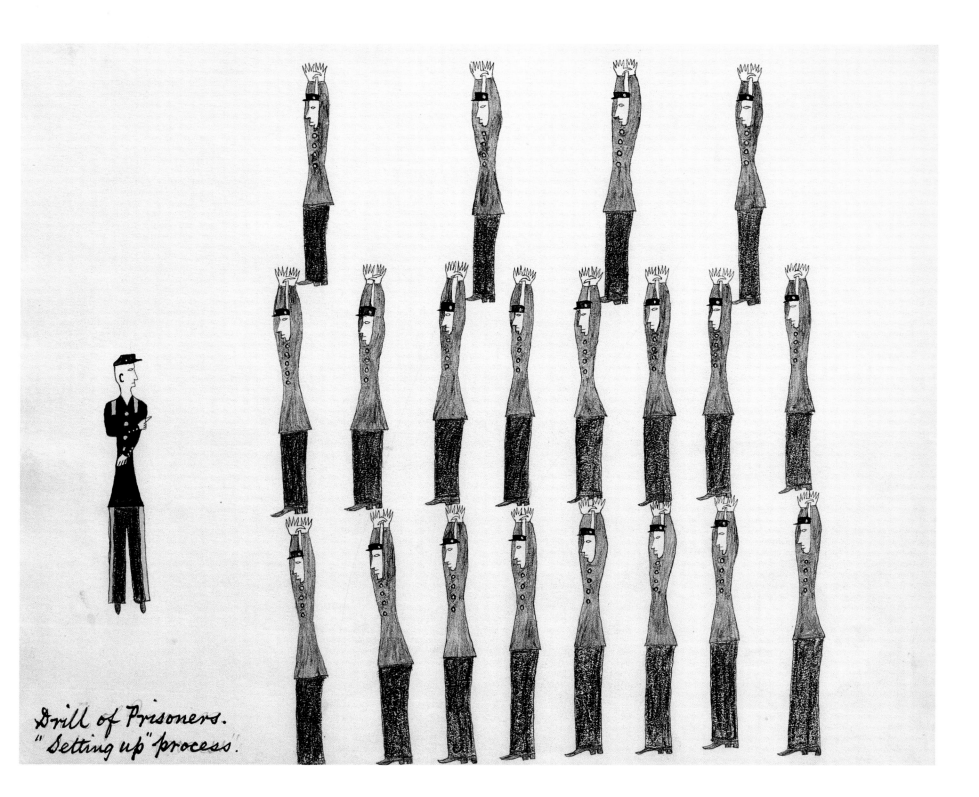

Drill of Prisoners.
"Setting up" process.

Target practice

Ft. Marion. Fla.

TARGET PRACTICE FT MARION. FLA

The Fort Marion prisoners gave archery demonstrations for visitors and also offered them lessons. Zotom depicts one of the young men passing a hat for donations as payment for the demonstration. According to an article in *Harpers Weekly,* some of the most dedicated archery students were the volunteers who taught them English. "In return for the kindness shown them by these excellent ladies, the Indians instruct them in archery, in the practice of which they are becoming very expert."

A related article in the Jacksonville *Tri-Weekly* suggests that the sport provided the Indians amusement as well as exercise. While receiving basic instructions, Hallie Parson, a Jacksonville resident, sent an arrow whizzing in the wrong direction. She heard a "Yelp" and then found herself surrounded by Indians. "I tell you," she admitted, "I was no little frightened until they all called out, 'Good, much good, white woman shoot Indian!'" At that moment a man appeared with the arrow sticking in the side of his tunic. "I don't know whether it went into his body or only his shirt," the novice archer confessed. "In fact, I was not particular enough to stop and enquire. Bidding Woman Heart and Mamanti (the chief I got the bow from) good-bye, I took my departure."

BISHOP WHIPPLE TALKING TO PRISONERS
FEB. & MARCH 1876

Zotom and Making Medicine each contributed his own version of a Fort Marion religious service to this ledger book indicating how important Christian instruction had become to them.

Making Medicine shows Bishop Whipple preaching to 45 attentive prisoners, while George Fox translates in sign language. Whipple was well liked by the Indians, and he became one of their biggest boosters, extolling their accomplishments to humanitarians, clergy, and government officials alike. "I have been at this place for my health and have been much interested in the Indian prisoners at Fort Marion," he wrote to President Ulysses S. Grant in March 1876. "The Indians came here sullen & defiant. …All were brought in irons. …A school was opened," he noted. "Some noble Christian women volunteered as teachers. The Indians have made good progress in learning to read & write. They have been taught the Lord's prayer & sing some Christian hymns very sweetly. They have non-commissioned officers of their own people, act as sentinels in charge of the fort, …and I doubt if there is a garrison in the land where the soldiers are more obedient & circumspect. When you remember that a few months ago these men were engaged in war…it touches the heart to see them sitting at the feet of women as docile children. I am sure that when they go back to their people they will be leaders in the work of civilization."

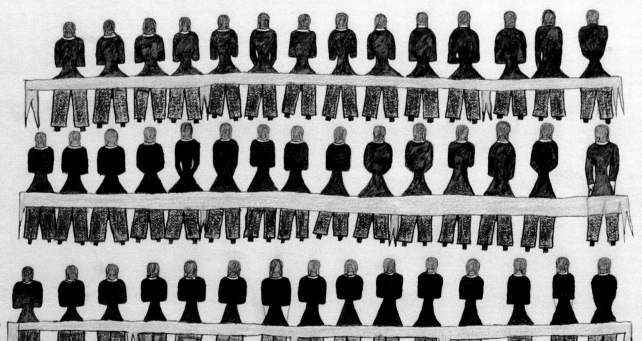

Bishop Whipple
talking to Prisoners
Feby & Mch. 1876

ACKNOWLEDGMENTS

All of us who cherish the artistic accomplishments of the Fort Marion artists owe a debt of gratitude to the descendants of former Commissioner of Indian Affairs John Q. Smith for having preserved this remarkable set of drawings for more than a century. I am especially grateful to the current owners, Hillary and Megan Thompson, his great, great, great granddaughters, for sharing their family treasure with the American public.

I am also indebted to Joseph D. Horse Capture for writing the captions for the Making Medicine drawings; to his father George P. Horse Capture, for his insightful comments on the introduction and captions; and to Sheila M. Mutchler, who brought these drawings to my attention. Thanks are also due to Robert M. Kvasnicka of the National Archives and Records Administration and William Eames, who helped with much of the research. I also wish to thank for their help Ralph E. Ehrenberg, Chief of the Geography and Map Division, Library of Congress; Robert A. Fliegel, Chief of Administration, and Clara Waldhari, Archivist, at the Castillo de San Marcos National Monument; Mary K. Herron, St. Augustine Historical Society; Vyrtis Thomas, National Anthropological Archives and William L. Withuhn, Curator of Transportation, National Museum of American History, Smithsonian Institution; Rhoda Ratner and Mayda R. Riopedre, Smithsonian Institution Libraries; John Kuss, New York Historical Society; Carol Verble, Missouri Historical Society; Alvin O. Turner, biographer of Making Medicine; Muriel Y. McDowell, Middle Georgia Regional Library, Macon; Dennis Limberhand, Lame Deer, Montana; and Kevin J. Mulroy, Kevin G. Craig, and Lisa Lytton-Smith, National Geographic Society.

HERMAN J. VIOLA

CONTRIBUTING AUTHORS

HERMAN J. VIOLA is curator emeritus at the Smithsonian Institution and a former director of its National Anthropological Archives. He is also the author of *After Columbus: The Smithsonian Chronicle of the North American Indians* and other works on Native Americans and the Far West.

JOSEPH D. HORSE CAPTURE is Assistant Curator of Africa, Oceania, and the Americas at the Minneapolis Institute of Arts.
GEORGE P. HORSE CAPTURE is Deputy Assistant Director for Cultural Resources at the National Museum of the American Indian.

BIBLIOGRAPHY

The information used in Warrior Artists came primarily from two sources, Richard Henry Pratt's memoirs, Battlefield and Classroom: Four Decades with the American Indian, 1867-1904, edited by Robert M. Utley and published by Yale University Press (1964), and records relating to the Bureau of Indian Affairs and Department of War in the custody of the National Archives. Particularly useful was the "Special File" titled "Indian Prisoners, Oct. 1874-Aug. 1875," of the Headquarters Division of the Missouri, Relating to Military Operations and Administration, 1863-1885. Many of Pratt's official reports about the Indians used in the introduction are printed in his memoirs.

In addition to newspaper accounts from the various cities through which the prisoners travelled on their way to Florida, the following publications were also helpful in writing the introduction and captions:

Berlo, Janet Catherine, ed. *Plains Indian Drawings, 1865-1935: Pages from Visual History.* New York: Harry N. Abrams, 1996.

Grinnell, George Bird. *The Cheyenne Indians, Their History and Way of Life.* 2 vols. New Haven: Yale University Press, 1923; reprinted ed., Lincoln: University of Nebraska Press, 1972.

Maurer, Evan M., ed. *Visions of the People: A Pictorial History of Plains Indian Life.* Minneapolis Institute of Arts and University of Washington Press, 1992.

Peterson, Karen Daniels. *Plains Indian Art from Fort Marion.* Norman: University of Oklahoma Press, 1971.

Powell, Peter J. *People of the Sacred Mountain, A History of the Cheyenne Chiefs and Warrior Societies, 1830-1878 with Epilogue 1969-1974.* 2 vols. San Francisco: Harper and Row, 1981.

Szabo, Joyce M. *Howling Wolf and the History of Ledger Art.* Albuquerque: University of New Mexico Press, 1994.

Turner, Alvin O., "Journey to Sainthood: David Pendleton Oakerhater's Better Way," Chronicles of Oklahoma, Vol. 70, No. 2 (Summer 1992), 116-142.

STAFF CREDITS

PUBLISHED BY THE NATIONAL GEOGRAPHIC SOCIETY

John H. Fahey, Jr., *President and Chief Executive Officer*
Gilbert M. Grosvenor, *Chairman of the Board*
Nina D. Hoffman, *Senior Vice President*

PREPARED BY THE BOOK DIVISION

William R. Gray, *Vice President and Director*
Charles Kogod, *Assistant Director*
Barbara A. Payne, *Editorial Director*
David Griffin, *Design Director*

STAFF FOR THIS BOOK:

Kevin J. Mulroy, *Project Editor*
Lisa Lytton-Smith, *Art Director*
Bonnie S. Lawrence, *Consulting Editor*
Kevin G. Craig, *Assistant Editor*
Peggy J. Candore, *Staff Assistant*

MANUFACTURING AND QUALITY CONTROL

George V. White, *Director*
John T. Dunn, *Associate Director*
Vincent P. Ryan, *Manager*
Polly P. Tompkins, *Executive Assistant*

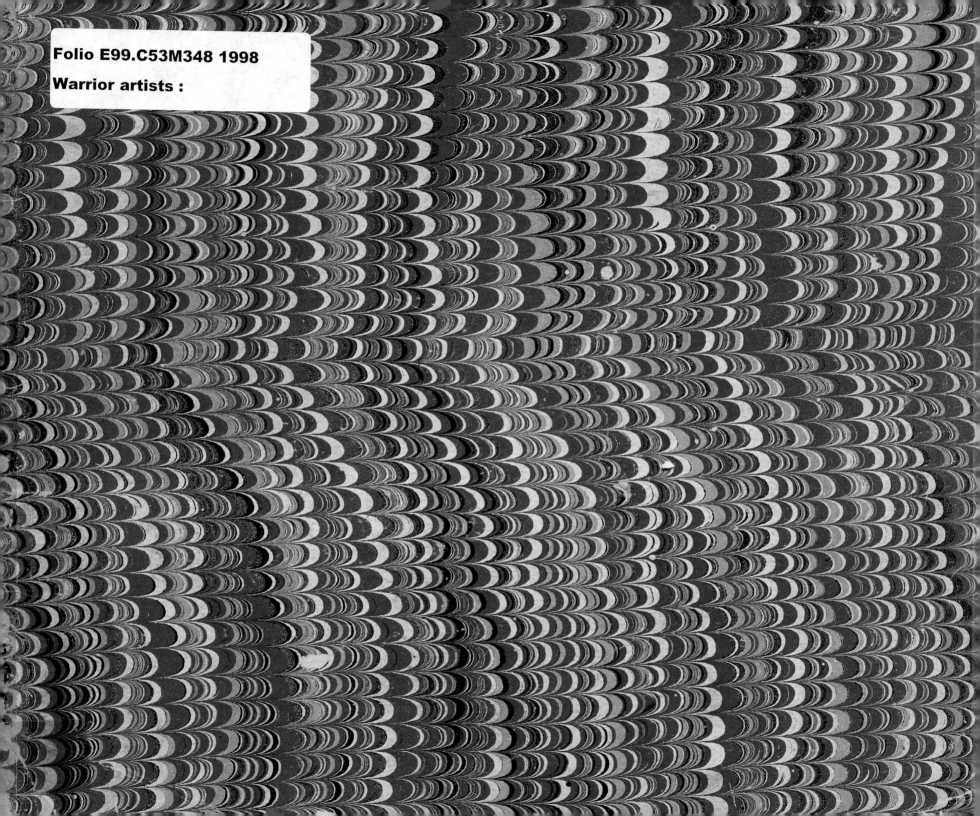